CLUB SUICIDE

Understanding Life After Suicide

by C. Rich

PROLOGUE

Today is a day like any other day. My awareness is full circle. Scratching away at my very soul. The evils which I now know. The terrible sight that I've seen. In the darkest corners of the world. In the most bottomless pits of despair. The four corners of nowhere. All the good things are canceled. My heart is nestled. Hanging on a fine thread, me.

I wrote those words long ago after my brother killed himself. What happened so long ago is like yesterday in my mind's eye. Many of you reading these words know exactly what I mean. Many are just now facing the horror of it. Many have faced this horror show more than once. We are part of a club. A club no one ever wants to be in. We are the survivors of suicide. We are the people left behind in the wake of unending despair. We stand witness to one of the most devastating acts a human being can do.

Strangely, when most people think of suicide, they think it is an act someone does to themselves. Ironically, nothing can be further from the truth. I believe life has called upon me to write a book about this subject. Whether that voice I hear pushing me towards this is just my subconscious calling out to me. Or maybe it is just the ones I once knew calling out to me from the grave regretting what they did. Somehow, I feel that I need to write this book. If not for me, but for the countless many out there of whom only they can understand.

The horrible truth is, if you are not in this club, you simply cannot understand. It is not something you can learn, but something you can only experience. It is something I would not wish on my worst enemy. I want to explain what it has been like for me. I want to tell you about my brother Keith and my friend Anthony along the way. I need to get this off my chest.

CHAPTER ONE

In 1989 I was at the precipice of adulthood. I was twenty years old. Not yet a man and not even old enough to have a cocktail legally. I had been dating this woman who was a year younger than me. The relationship was getting serious. Now being raised Irish Catholic, what this meant was it was time to bring the lady home to meet Mom. That is a big event in a young man's life. Bringing home a woman for your mother to meet for the first time signaled that it was now becoming a real relationship.

A typical Irish mother will take this time to embarrass the hell out of you with old pictures and tattletales of your youth. She, more times than not, has a field day throwing you under the bus and telling the girl to run as fast as she can away from this danger she calls her son. For ages, Irish mothers have been taught this skill from a young age. They pass down this tradition from one generation of fiery women to the next and mine was no different.

I drove my lady down from North Broward County, Florida to the southern tip of the county to a town called Miramar, Florida. We arrived at my mother's house. The house I grew up in. I parked the car in the driveway like I had done a million times before.

We went in and the evening began. This was the first time my girlfriend had ever been to my childhood home. She was looking at the pictures, sports trophies, and ribbons displayed across the fireplace. I'm sure she was nervous; I don't think any guy before I did such a thing with meeting the mother so formerly with her.

We all sat down around the dining room table. It was a classic old wood-style dining room with a beautiful breakfront filled with china and fancy glasses. The night was going along just fine until there was a knock at the door. I got up from the table and walked across the house to answer the knock. When I opened the door there were two police officers standing on my mother's porch and they asked to come in. Now normally, in the Walker House, the answer is always no to that question. My mother had three boys and it was not uncommon to have knocks on the door from law enforcement. Her boys were rough on our hometown to say it mildly. For a good portion of our lives growing up, my mother was a single mom whose three boys pretty much ran wild from sunrise to sunset.

Standing there in the doorway, I could tell this was a completely different tone and I let them in. They asked my mother if she was the mother of my brother Keith, and they told her to please have a seat. Just the way they said it, somehow, we instinctively knew. Before the cops could say another word, my mother let out a scream. I can tell you; I know of no words in the dictionary to describe this scream. I never heard anything like that before. It still echoes in my head after all these decades. At the time it went through my bones, it thundered through my entire body and soul. My legs gave out upon hearing it and I fell against the wall and just slid down it slowly. My girlfriend tried to lift me back up, but my legs were not under me anymore. I just could not feel them. I lay there against the wall in front of the fireplace in our main living room listening to the cops tell my mom that my brother shot himself in the city of Plantation, Florida at his girlfriend's house. My brother was sixteen years old, and he killed himself over a girl. I could not believe the brother who I grew up with was dead. My brother who came down from New York City with my family to start a new life in Florida was now gone. I just went numb.

 I told the cops, "Get a priest here now!" and they walked outside to make that happen.

I didn't know what to do. I didn't know what to say. I just knew we needed to pray. My family went to St. Bartholomew in Miramar our whole lives, but for some reason, no one answered the phone at the time when the police called. They landed up calling another Catholic Church in our town called St. Stephens and they sent a priest over right away.

When the priest showed up we all sat around the table holding hands and praying. I cannot imagine what this might have felt like to my girlfriend and soon-to-be wife at the time. The priest spoke about how we are starting to realize that suicide is a sickness and that the people who do this should be treated like they have a disease. I was furious! It was the 1980s and we were not at any level of enlightenment on the subject of suicide. We were taught as Catholics, that suicide was a mortal sin and that we went straight to Hell after we committed this sin. I got so angry and started to yell at the priest.

I said, "You are here, so we can all pray for my brother who is in Hell right now!"

I screamed, "You are here, so we can get God's attention and get my brother out of those flames!"

Looking back at it I was completely out of my mind in unspeakable grief. You see I was not ready to throw out my entire belief system of everything I had been taught all my life, just because my brother screwed up and committed a mortal sin.

You see one of the things about suicide is that it challenges your relationship with God right away. Suicide throws you right into a direct battle with God.

You scream, "Why!"

You plead, "Why him or her?"

You cannot understand how this can be God's plan. You question why God is punishing your family or allowing this to happen. You stand before your Creator in an epic battle for your faith and for your very relationship with God.

If you are a person who has never experienced this, it is hard to convey, but all I can say is, I have never been angrier at God than I was back during the first stages of this horrific event. At that moment, if God was going to let my brother burn in Hell, then I and God had a huge problem. I was going to go to bat for my brother and battle the Almighty if I had to!

Suicide rocks your faith in God down to its very core. Almost everyone turns their back on God at this moment, even if it is only for a second in time. Some never return to God. Everything about what you know and who you are gets questioned. Nothing tests your experience here on Earth more than having a close family member kill themselves.

If suicide could be compared to an onion, I would say that it has more layers. That it is an unending or perennial set of consequences that never seems to stop unfolding for the rest of a survivor's life.

The method by which a person kills themselves is one of the first layers to deal with. There are many ways to commit suicide and human beings keep perfecting more ways to do it as I get older. My brother killed himself by placing a pistol on his chest and blowing away his heart. That is a very American way to commit suicide and mostly how men do it.

Women have an altogether different set of methods to do the same act. The family left behind envisions how their loved one died and what their last moments were. We ponder whether or not our loved one felt pain or not. We wonder what was their last thoughts. The method of how somebody kills themselves leaves a scar on the soul and memory of the people left behind. The actual method used is part of the memory of the whole event. We all hope it was quick and painless. However, in truth, the people that do this are racked with pain. For them, suicide was their painkiller.

CHAPTER TWO

The initial shock of a close family member's suicide is complicated by the funeral that often follows. Because of the nature of a suicide death, it is unlike any other funeral. People in general do not know what to say or how to act at a suicide funeral. Many families do not have a service because of the circumstance of the death, but many do.

My family went forward with a funeral that became one of the worst memories of my life. Just the act of calling around the country to relatives and explaining what happened is a horrific event on its own. One call after the other explaining what transpired, was salt on the emotional wound. How many times over the phone can you muster up the proper emotion to say such a thing to people? It almost becomes robotic and that becomes its own scar. Many things happen at normal funerals that stress a family.

In my case, my mother was completely inconsolable. You could not even speak to her. I never saw anyone so racked with grief in all my life. For a parent, it hits them the hardest. To see your own child, take their life, is a pain that not even the English dictionary has a word for. Our lexicon falls short of providing the proper adjective to describe it. My mother slipped into a dark place where no one could reach her. Being the eldest, I felt obligated to just provide a perimeter fence around her to protect her from people and their awkward responses. This was a situation my family was ill-equipped for.

No one I know has a prepaid cemetery plot for a child. We certainly didn't. In a pinch, my father's mother gave up her plot, next to her husband, already waiting for her in a cemetery in Davie, Florida.

My entire family on both sides came from New York City. Irish New Yorkers are not generally known for serene funerals. As my family started to arrive from out of the state, my mother barricaded herself in her bedroom. I had a brand-new stepfather at the time, and he stayed in the room consoling Mom. They asked me to take care of everyone in the house.

In a horrible string of events, my grandfather found a mason jar of moonshine that was kept on top of the refrigerator. To my utter horror, my mother remarried a Florida Cracker and redneck type, who kept such a jar in the kitchen. Grandpa was an old-school alcoholic who did better on beer than booze. He certainly was not the type to indulge in redneck moonshine. Grandpa made the choice of drinking this powerful liquid madness and madness is what we got.

While my mother stayed in her bedroom, Grandpa was raging through the house and slapping around Grandma. Now this was not the first time Grandpa put his hands on Grandma. They came from a generation where this kind of behavior was commonplace. Many men of their generation would get boozed up and start slapping their wives around. The social traditions at the time dictated that it was not anyone's business.

However, it became my business when my mother called me into her room and told me to handle Grandpa and get control of the house. Now my grandfather was one of the toughest guys I ever knew. He was looked upon like that from the whole neighborhood back in the city. People knew, not to mess with this guy. Now I was young and full of beans and knew I was in a pickle. I had to confront my grandfather and get him to stop or leave the house. When I confronted him in his moonshine fog, he started screaming at me. He yelled that he gave me a place to live before when I was a baby and when my father failed to keep a roof over my head. Grandpa screamed out all of the things he had done for me in my life. I told him he had to leave, and he gathered up grandma and left screaming and yelling profanities at me. I was just grateful I did not have to fight him.

You see suicide makes people act strange. Grandpa knew not to touch that moonshine. He also knew it was a way to escape the real feelings and situations we all found ourselves in. Looking back now, no one was at their best.

The day of the funeral came. We had the funeral at Fred Hunter's Funeral Home and one by one people showed up awkwardly not knowing how to act or what to say. My father and mother who had been divorced could not grieve together for the loss of their kid due to my mom's new husband and the weird dynamics that surrounded that. My brother's girlfriend showed up which filled me with much anger and mixed emotions. To think that the last minutes of my brother's life were shared by someone who only knew him for a matter of months aggregated my anger even more. I remember just being filled with so much anger that day. Then my brother's NA friends started showing up. For some unexplainable reason, my brother started hanging out and going to Narcotics Anonymous meetings even though he did not do drugs. It was a very strange thing. These NA people showed up and started putting NA stuff into the casket with my brother's body. I almost lost my mind and went crazy on them, but my mother said it was OK because these were his friends. They filled up my brother's casket with NA medallions and stuff to the point that my brother's casket became some NA Time Capsule that should be dug up years later or something. I was furious about the disrespect that was going on. The horrible wake ended, and we all went to the cemetery to say our last goodbyes as my brother got lowered into the ground next to my father's father. It was just a bad day all around. I later returned to the grave all by myself with a bottle of booze and sat there drinking and talking to my brother. I was so lost at the time. I yelled at God while sitting there at my brother's grave and I said the most horrible things to God. It took me years to even pray again. For me, my faith was shattered. I could not wrap my brain around what happened to my family. Between my parents' divorce and my brother's suicide, my sense of family was eviscerated forever. To this day, I have no feeling of family when it comes to those of us who were related to each other. Thirty-some-odd years later while writing this book, I still have no sense of family with my relatives. Suicide had an unending negative effect on me as a human being. I have never lost that sense of anger and sadness inside. It consumed me, the essence of me. I can still feel the stain of anger and sadness from the loss of my family. I am unable to interact with my family normally. They are all just reminders of things I'd just rather forget.

CHAPTER THREE

When it comes to suicide in the 21st century, there seems to be an uptick in its occurrence. As globalization and technology grow, more and more people are cut out of the economy and left with nothing. No job, no skills for the modern world and many already lost their home in the economic crash of 2008. Between that and the endless wars laid upon our military families, suicide has taken on a new face. Take all those factors and then include suicide bombers in the Islamic world, murder-suicides, and behold, we have a new culture of death and destruction. A culture where it becomes commonplace to hear about one form of suicide after the other daily. A culture of death has sprung up in the beginning part of the 21st Century, forcing the rest of us to face unthinkable horrors.

According to save.org, these were the statics at the time I started writing this book:

SAVE uses the most current data available from the Centers for Disease Control and Prevention.   In 2014, there were 42,773 deaths by suicide in the United States. Suicide is the 10th leading cause of death; homicide ranks 17th. It is the second leading cause of death for 15 - 24-year-olds. Click on the chart to the right which shows the Ten Leading Causes of Death in the U.S. in 2014. For more data, you may visit www.cdc.gov or www.who.int. For more comprehensive data, visit the CDC website's Web-based Injury Statistics Query and Reporting System (WISQARS)

General Statistics

Suicide is the 10th leading cause of death in the US for all ages. (CDC)

The suicide rates decreased from 1990-2000 from 12.5 suicides per 100,000 to 10.4 per 100,000. Over the past decade, however, the rate has again increased to 12.1 per 100,000. Every day, approximately 105 Americans die by suicide. (CDC)

There is one death by suicide in the US every 12.3 minutes. (CDC)

Depression affects 20-25% of Americans ages 18+ in a given year. (CDC)

Suicide takes the lives of over 38,000 Americans every year. (CDC)

Only half of all Americans experiencing an episode of major depression receive treatment. (NAMI)

80% -90% of adolescents that seek treatment for depression are treated successfully using therapy and/or medication. (TADS study)

An estimated quarter million people each year become suicide survivors (AAS).

There is one suicide for every estimated 25 suicide attempts. (CDC)

There is one suicide for every estimated 4 suicide attempts in the elderly. (CDC)

Gender Disparities

Suicide among males is 4x's higher than among females. Male deaths represent 79% of all US suicides. (CDC)

Firearms are the most commonly used method of suicide among males (51%). (CDC)

Access to firearms is associated with a significantly increased risk of suicide. (NAMI)

Females are more likely than males to have had suicidal thoughts. (CDC)

Females experience depression at roughly 2x's the rate of men. (SMH)

Females attempt suicide 3x's as often as males. (CDC)

Poisoning is the most common method of suicide for females. (CDC)

Age Disparities

1 in 100,000 children ages 10 to 14 die by suicide each year. (NIMH)

7 in 100,000 youth ages 15 to 19 die by suicide each year. (NIMH)

12.7 in 100,000 young adults ages 20-24 die by suicide each year. (NIMH)

The prevalence of suicidal thoughts, suicidal planning, and suicide attempts is significantly higher among adults aged 18-29 than among adults aged 30+. (CDC)

Suicide is the 2nd leading cause of death for 15- to 24-year-old Americans. (CDC)

Suicide is the 4th leading cause of death for adults ages 18-65. (CDC)

The highest increase in suicide is in males 50+ (30 per 100,000). (CDC)

Suicide rates for females are highest among those aged 45-54 (9 per 100,000). (CDC)

Suicide rates for males are highest among those aged 75+ (36 per 100,000). (CDC)

Suicide rates among the elderly are highest for those who are divorced or widowed. (SMH)

Racial and Ethnic Disparities

The highest suicide rates in the US are among Whites, American Indians, and Alaska Natives.

Worldwide

Over 800,000 people die by suicide every year. (WHO)

There is one death by suicide in the world every 40 seconds. (WHO)

Suicide is the 3rd leading cause of death in the world for those aged 15-44 years. (WHO)

Depression is the leading cause of disability worldwide. (WHO)

When looking at those numbers one can only gasp in complete horror. When suicide makes it into the top ten ways people are dying, we have a problem. Just looking at the list of famous people who committed suicide on Wikipedia and one can see another glaring reminder of this ongoing struggle become apparent.

Wikipedia:

https://en.wikipedia.org/wiki/List_of_suicides
As of 4/18/16

Furthermore, I can provide you with some general statistics on suicide in the United States as of 2022. Please note that these figures are based on data available up to my knowledge cutoff date in September 2021, and there may have been updates or changes since then. Here are some key statistics related to suicide in the U.S.:

1. **Overall Suicide Rates:**
   - In 2020, the age-adjusted suicide rate in the United States was 14.5 per 100,000 individuals.
   - The total number of suicides in 2020 was approximately 44,834.

2. **Age and Gender:**
   - Suicide rates tend to vary by age and gender. Historically, men have had higher suicide rates than women. In 2020, the suicide rate for males was 22.7 per 100,000, while for females, it was 6.2 per 100,000.
   - The age group with the highest suicide rate in 2020 was individuals aged 45-54.

3. **Methods:**
   - Firearms are the most common method of suicide in the United States. In 2019, nearly 50% of all suicide deaths involved firearms.
   - Other common methods include suffocation/hanging and poisoning.

4. **Occupational Breakdown:**
   - Certain occupations have been associated with higher suicide rates. Occupations that involve high levels of stress, access to

lethal means, and limited social support may be at greater risk.

- Occupations such as healthcare workers, first responders (police officers, firefighters, and paramedics), and military personnel have been noted to have elevated suicide rates.

5. **Veterans:**

- Suicide rates among U.S. military veterans have been a concern. The U.S. Department of Veterans Affairs reported that in 2019, an average of 17.6 veterans died by suicide each day.

6. **Racial and Ethnic Disparities:**

- Suicide rates can vary among different racial and ethnic groups. Historically, white individuals have had higher suicide rates compared to Black and Hispanic individuals.

7. **Prevention Efforts:**

- Suicide prevention is a critical public health issue. Various organizations and initiatives are dedicated to raising awareness, providing support, and promoting mental health.

It's important to note that suicide is a complex and multifaceted issue influenced by a wide range of factors, including mental health, social and economic circumstances, access to mental healthcare, and cultural attitudes. If you are conducting research on this topic, I encourage you to explore the factors contributing to suicide, preventive measures, and interventions to support those at risk.

For the most up-to-date and accurate information, I recommend referring to official sources such as the Centers for Disease Control and Prevention (CDC) and other reputable research institutions.

CHAPTER FOUR

The incontestable intertwinement of religion, faith, and the subject of suicide brings with it its own burdens. The world religions for the longest time were not so enlightened about the subject of killing oneself. In fact, they were downright brutal. Kill yourself and you went to Hell without passing go. There was no spot on the Monopoly Board of Life for this act.

In Judaism, a suicide is buried in another part of the cemetery. They are also denied certain burial rights. However, some suicides are acceptable in Jewish Law. The famous story of Mass suicide by a group of Jews called the Sicarii on the mountaintop fortress of Masada is just one example. Nine hundred and Sixty Jews killed themselves down to the last person to avoid being enslaved by the Romans. That story is almost a tale of Jewish pride.

Even the strictest form of Christianity, the Roman Catholic Church, has softened its stance on suicide. They acknowledge this is breaking one of the Ten Commandments, but still look for modern-day explanations in mental health to explain the act. When I was coming up as a child they would not even provide a Catholic Requiem (Funeral Mass) or a cemetery plot for someone who killed themselves. Now they reach for excuses like grave psychological disturbances, anguish, or grave fear of hardship, suffering, or torture when coming to justifying or explaining the responsibility of the one committing suicide.

Islam ironically bans suicide clearly and is still old school with "Whoever kills himself, intentionally, he will be in the fire of hell for eternity."

The eastern Dharmic religions such as Hinduism, Jainism, and Buddhism say that suicide has a cause and effect on one's next life or rebirth.

Hinduism for example accepts a man's right to end one's life through the non-violent practice of fasting to death. This act is called Prayopavesa. However, Prayopavesa is only allowed for old-age yogis who have no desire or ambition left in life, and no responsibilities remaining to others. A second example is committing suicide in a battle to save one's honor.

Jainism considers suicide the highest form of violence and forbids it. However, they too have this fasting-to-death honor, but they call it sallekhanā.

Buddhism heavily leans on Karma with its reincarnation cycles and frowns upon suicide. In the Encyclopedia of Religion, Marilyn J. Harran wrote the following:

"Buddhism in its various forms affirms that, while suicide as self-sacrifice may be appropriate for the person who is an arhat, one who has attained enlightenment, it is still very much the exception to the rule."

However, those exceptions do exist. I even found a couple of exceptions listed in Wikipedia. According to that source:

One exception is the Buddhist tale of a bhikkhu named Vakkali who was extremely ill and racked with excruciating pain. He was said to have committed suicide when near death and upon making statements suggesting he had passed beyond desires (and thus perhaps an Arhant). Self-euthanasia appears as the context for his death.

Another exception is the story of a bhikkhu named Godhika, also beset by illness, who had repeatedly attained temporary liberation of mind but was unable to gain final liberation due to illness. While believing himself again in a state of temporary liberation it occurred to him to cut his own throat, in hopes thus to be reborn in a high realm.

Even Neopagan Religions such as Wicca are vague and contradictory towards the subject of suicide.

So, as you can see when one leans on religion for answers in what to think or how to act, over suicide, it becomes even more unclear.

CHAPTER FIVE

Now every suicide is different for the people left behind. In most cases, there were signs of trouble before the act happened. Red flags one can look back at and point to. However, it is rare that sometimes there are no signs at all and people are left stunned and caught off guard. I tend to think in such cases people were just simply missing the signs and that there is at least one person who saw trouble ahead. In my case, there was a lifetime of signs and trouble with my brother Keith. Things were wrong in his head from a very early age. I believe he was broken from birth and as the years unfolded we got to see one glaring sign after the other that we had a problem.

As my brother got older, he started to become more violent. My mother would put him in one mental hospital after the other and most times their staff there would land up in the Emergency room due to the violence my brother exacted on them. By the time he was sixteen years old even my mother was afraid he was going to kill her. I damn sure feared it. His odious and precarious behavior kept escalating. Each year my brother would attack me to show he can beat me in a fight. As he got stronger and stronger I realized that one day he would overcome me. He was getting far too strong for me to subdue him. The task became harder and harder. I was left as the protector of my mom and the family. My stepfather had already thrown him out of the house we grew up in by the age of fifteen.

The last battle I had with my brother was epic. I was no longer living at my childhood home and I got a call from my step-sister that lived on the beach in Hallandale, Florida. Her mother was on the phone asking me to come get my brother. I was told that my brother rapped our step-sister and was just sitting on the couch and would not leave. Her mother was trying to get the tampon out of her daughter's vagina that my brother had stuffed up in her during the rape. I jumped in my car in the middle of the night and drove as fast as I could to the high-rise where they lived at. I went upstairs and went into the apartment and got my brother out of there. In the elevator going down to the ground floor where my car was my brother stood there silent. I asked him if it was true and he told me, "Of course it is!" We got down into the lobby of the building and I grabbed his arm to pull him towards my car. He recoiled and started yelling out at me that I was going to tell Mom and how the bitch deserved it. I got him in the backseat of my car and locked him in. I had an Audi at the time that allowed me to control the door locks from the front seat. As I drove over the bridge that went over the intercostal waterway, my brother started screaming and thrashing about in the backseat. Once we realized he could not open the door, he started to blast out my windows with his feet. I stopped the car on the top of the bridge on Hallandale Beach Blvd. and Keith crawled out of the window. I darted out of my car on top of the bridge and tackled him. In one of the worst fights, I have ever been in I fought my brother on top of that bridge for twenty minutes at 3 AM in the morning. I fought him to near exhaustion. He was just getting too strong for me. It took me twenty minutes to subdue him and I have no idea how a cop did not drive by the whole time. As I started to bring him back to the car he broke away and started running towards the end of the bridge. In what seemed like slow motion my brother went to jump from the bridge. We were on top of this bridge but just passed the water where the cement began. As he jumped over the rails I caught his ankles and his whole body went over and slammed back against the bridge. There I was in the middle of the night on top of a bridge holding on to my brother's ankles as he scratched away at the wall trying to pull himself down and away from me. To this day only God would be able to tell you how on Earth I still had enough energy and strength to pull him back over the wall and onto the bridge again. Somehow I did. He lay on the bridge crying, and I pulled into my car once again. I drove him straight to Hollywood Memorial and I had him Baker Acted into the mental ward. In Florida, The Baker Act is a law that you can commit someone who is a danger to themselves or others for seventy-two hours to be evaluated by a doctor. I got my brother taken care of and I had to drive back to my mother's home to wake her in the early morning hours to explain to her that one of her sons rapped her husband's daughter and was now committed in the mental hospital.

In the end, my stepfamily did not press charges against my brother, and he was dead from a self-inflicted gunshot wound not too long after that. I remember feeling incredible guilt that I was relieved he was dead. I just knew he was going to kill someone one day. I was actually grateful that he did not take anyone with him as he left this Earth. The guilt that comes with feeling this way blanketed my soul. How would I be relieved that my brother was dead? My mother at the time and a few time since has mentioned the same feelings. Something was wrong with my brother, one more year of life and I would have never been able to overcome his strength and protect anyone. He might have killed me. We never knew truly what was wrong with Keith. The medical field in the 1980s was horribly behind in this kind of brain science and psychiatry. There was something wrong with my brother's brain and we will never know what or why. One of the memories I had of this uncertainty was when my brother was very young, we had a neighbor across the street knock on our door. She asked me to come out to see what my brother did. Keith no older than five or six years old, had gone in our refrigerator and gotten a large jar of yellow mustard and a paintbrush. Keith painted our neighbor's entire Station wagon yellow. When I asked him why, he had no answer. I knew that very day, something was wrong with my brother.

CHAPTER SIX

There are many aspects of suicide I have no experience with and that I felt needed to be addressed. One is the act of someone witnessing a suicide. I never saw my brother kill himself and that is a whole category of suicide survivors that I know nothing of. Because I have no experience with something that horrific, people who did have my unending sympathy. If you went through such an ordeal my heart goes out to you. I did not witness my brother's suicide. I only witness an attempt and I stopped it. Like many others, people in pain make multiple attempts. My brother found his mark.

I remember not too long after my family was hit with this devastation I found myself in this restaurant. It was a log cabin type of place with a wooden porch and inside were long wooden tables and benches. The place was known for its Garlic Crabs. People sat at these long tables with large buckets in front of them filled with crabs just bathing in this beautiful garlic butter. There were wooden spools that lined the table with unlimited paper towels because cracking crabs got messy.

I was swimming in my garlicky heaven, and I excused myself to go to the restroom. As I walked through the place, I could hear a certain level of buzz that came from the people eating, drinking, and laughing. Moose heads and other unfortunate creatures lined the walls of the restaurant staff and mounted. When I entered the men's room the lighting in there was kind of dark. I could see that there was one of those old fashion toilets with a chain that you pull to flush. As I went over to the stall a man was in there washing his hands in the sink. As I started to unzip my pants he asked me, "Are you having a good day?" I was caught a little off guard because he was clearly breaking some unspoken rules and etiquette by engaging me in conversation. I look back at him through the dim light and answered, "Well…Yes, I am." I heard the water stop in the sink and the room became silent. In what sounded like a completely different voice I heard the words, "Well that is about to change."

By now I was in the middle of doing my business and my stream of urine cut off and I said, "Excuse me?" "What did you say?" I could never see his face properly in the dim light of the restroom and he walked out before answering me. My stream returned to its thrust and I just stood there wondering what the heck that was all about. When I was done I walked over to the sink to wash my hands when I saw words written on the mirror. The words said, MET ME OUTSIDE I KNOW YOUR BROTHER in bold caps. I stood there completely confused and looked down into the sink and there was blood all around the faucets and pooled at the bottom of this old fashion sink and mirror. I rubbed my index finger over the words written in the mirror and looked down at my finger. It looked like blood but I was not sure.

I walked back outside into the restaurant, and nobody was paying any attention to me or noticed the trail of trickling blood from the restroom door going out the front door of the crab cabin. I followed the spotted line of blood outside. It was evening time.

The sun was almost all the way down. I stood on the wooden porch where I could see that the blood trail ended once the wooden steps met the grass. The restaurant was deep in a wooded area. The land was cleared around the restaurant and all the trees were removed to make a parking lot. I could see the man that was in the restroom on the outskirt of the clearing right at the edge of where the woods started again. He turned around and looked at me and then walked into the deep forest. It was an eerie thing to see because I had no idea where he was going. It was almost dark and as far as I knew there was nothing but woods for miles around. As I turned around on the restaurant's porch and started to walk back inside a little girl walked up to me and pulled on my shirt. She said, "This is for you" and handed me a piece of paper. She told me the man with the mean face told me to give it to you. I asked what man and she pointed towards the woods where I watched the guy walk into the trees. I looked down and opened the paper but I could not read it in the night light that was available from the sky. I placed the paper in my pocket and returned to the benches and resumed my place at the table in front of my heavenly bucket of Garlic Crabs. As I sat there cracking my crabs, I wondered what the heck was going on with that dude. Soon conversation at the table swept my thoughts up and another direction and I soon forgot all about the man in the restroom. Later that night when I got home I was getting undressed and I reached into my pocket to empty my car keys and stuff on my nightstand when I pulled out the piece of paper the little girl gave me back at the restaurant. It all came rushing back to me and I remembered the strangeness earlier in the day at the Crab Cabin. I opened the piece of paper and read the words written in large caps.

"YOUR BROTHER IS NOT DEAD"

I woke up screaming. I realized that this whole ordeal at the restaurant was a dream. I was grateful that it did not happen, and that it was not real. However, I apperceived at that moment that because of suicide, I was going to have a lifetime of nightmares. That wasn't going to be the last time I woke up in a pool of sweat. Suicide torches you while you are awake, and it follows you in your sleep. There is no escaping it, there is no running from it. This is one of those things the person who commits suicide leaves behind. It ripples through life like a stone thrown into a pond.

CHAPTER SEVEN

According to the Mayo Clinic: Suicide warning signs or suicidal thoughts include:

Talking about suicide — for example, making statements such as "I'm going to kill myself," "I wish I were dead" or "I wish I hadn't been born"

Getting the means to take your own life, such as buying a gun or stockpiling pills

Withdrawing from social contact and wanting to be left alone

Having mood swings, such as being emotionally high one day and deeply discouraged the next

Being preoccupied with death, dying or violence

Feeling trapped or hopeless about a situation

Increasing use of alcohol or drugs

Changing normal routine, including eating or sleeping patterns

Doing risky or self-destructive things, such as using drugs or driving recklessly

Giving away belongings or getting affairs in order when there's no other logical explanation for doing this

Saying goodbye to people as if they won't be seen again

Developing personality changes or being severely anxious or agitated, particularly when experiencing some of the warning signs listed above

Warning signs aren't always obvious, and they may vary from person to person. Some people make their intentions clear, while others keep suicidal thoughts and feelings secret.

Suicidal thoughts have many causes. Most often, suicidal

thoughts are the result of feeling like you can't cope when you're faced with what seems to be an overwhelming life situation. If you don't have hope for the future, you may mistakenly think suicide is a solution. You may experience a sort of tunnel vision, where in the middle of a crisis you believe suicide is the only way out.

There also may be a genetic link to suicide. People who complete suicide or who have suicidal thoughts or behavior are more likely to have a family history of suicide.

I am no professional when it comes to suicide. If you are feeling like you want to die or you know someone, you need to call the proper professionals. I am however one who has had direct interaction with a suicide survivor. I have seen what it has done to the family who were left behind. I have felt its unending effects on my life directly and indirectly. I am of the opinion that the closer you were to the person that committed this act, the more harmful it is to the induvial left behind. The effect of suicide unfolds well past the date of death. For me, it has been a burden that has damaged my relationship with the world around me. Over time and frank discussions between me and others, I have survived it. While writing this book, I have learned much about myself as well. I was startled by the latest statics. Suicide wasn't something people did to themselves; it was done to all of us left behind.

CHAPTER EIGHT

Later in my adult life, I was lucky enough to have a mentor. I worked for an Italian Food Wholesaler. I spent six years of my life driving a food service truck and delivering all the food to Italian and Greek restaurants exclusively. It seemed like a normal job from the outside. However, from the inside world of food distribution and from the view of hanging on a cheese truck, there was nothing normal about it whatsoever. It was an Italian thing. Whether it was the olive oil companies out of Italy called the Agra - Mafia and their shenanigans or the many pizzerias owned by retired and not so retired gangsters, the world of mozzarella cheese was as colorful.

The education I got about how our food chain in America works was priceless. What was also priceless was a good stick of cheese. The mozzarella cheese was shaped into blocks that looked like gold bars and as far as the restaurateurs were concerned, it is bouillon, plain and simple. The tug of war over these gold bars amongst the Italians with the buying and selling of it rivaled any Wall Street brokerage firm I had ever seen. The people behind the scenes looked like they were plucked right out of any one of the Mafia Movies we have all watched over the years. Cheese in America is big business, and the pricing of mozzarella cheese is nothing short of a blood sport. There is a never-ending, ongoing, and high-stakes trade war raging just under the nose of the American consumer without anyone knowing it. This was the world where I met my mentor, Anthony. Over the years he taught me everything I needed to know about that world.

Anthony's father started the companies in the 1930s and it was a family affair. The whole family was involved, and Anthony and his brothers ran the company. After their father passed away the brother took over everything and Anthony was the top dog owner. I did not meet him or work for him until the late 1990s. At that time Anthony lost the company to another group of Italians and was left in charge of running the daily operations.

I worked in that industry for many years. Anthony and I got really close during this time. We shared interests in lots of things including our love for the television show called The Sopranos. Ironically my stint at the company lasted the whole run of that iconic show. After I left the company, I went on to work in the field of information technology and I moved away.

Anthony and I kept in touch and spoke on the phone every week. Each Monday he would call me to talk about life and family. This went on for many years and we grew even closer. Anthony would tell me everything about his personal life and we would share all sorts of stuff together. Anthony was having a hard time with his marriage. From a distance, I could tell this was a very volatile couple and they fought quite a bit. I felt like I really knew this man and that he knew me better than most. One Monday Anthony never called. I did not think much of it at the time. Anthony would miss our Monday call from time to time. Next thing I know I got a call from his stepson who tells me that last Monday Anthony shot himself in the head, sitting in his car, in his own driveway at his house. I dropped the phone and started to scream and cry.

I could not believe my friend was dead. I couldn't believe he did it on "our" Monday. I did not understand why he did not just call me instead of doing such a thing. I wondered did I missed the call. I mused whether he needed me and whether I was not there for him. There I was dealing with another suicide in my life. Here I was drowning in a sea of despair once again. I was numb and in shock.

It has been many years since that day, but I think of my friend all the time. I miss him so much, especially on Mondays. Suicide is one of the most selfish things a person could do. This act is not about the person that commits it, it is about the people left behind. The unending pain that the survivors of suicide deal with is never really talked about. Only we in this club know this rippling sorrow, it is a horrible club to be in.

CHAPTER NINE

By the time I started writing this book in 2016 America's suicide rate had become alarming. "We're losing more people to suicide than breast cancer, car accidents, homicides," said Dr. Dan Reidenberg, the executive director of Save.org. "We'd be fortunate for other companies to get on the bandwagon."

After twelve years of what seemed like an unending war, the economic crash of 2008, and more and more people being left behind with fast-changing technology there seemed to be a hopelessness that was blanketing the nation.

I was even touched by suicide once again in June of 2016. After many years and thanks to Facebook, I reunited with a childhood friend of mine. After spending hours chatting and catching up on old times I walked around the rest of the week on a cloud of happiness. It was just good to reconnect with someone who was a big part of me growing up. After my brother's suicide, I left my home town never to return again. It was only through Facebook that I was able to reunite with all the people I grew up with and went to school. The same week I was walking around on cloud nine because of this reconnection with an old friend, I got a text from another childhood friend. The text on my phone said something had happened to our mutual friend and to go check Facebook. I did and I saw my childhood buddy's son had just taken his own life. I could not believe after all of this time, I finally hook back up with a friend the very week his son commits suicide. Top that off with the fact I was smack dab in the middle of writing a book on suicide and I felt like the universe was talking to me. I mean what are the odds of all that?

Then, that very same week on Tuesday, June 14, 2016, Facebook introduced new tools on its social network for suicide prevention. In the biggest step by a major technology company to incorporate suicide prevention tools into its platform, the social network introduced mechanisms and processes to make it easier for people to help friends who post messages about suicide or self-harm. It was like the universe was screaming for me to keep writing this book. Something was clearly changing. America was now at a thirty-year high for suicide. According to Mike Isaac and The New York Times, "With more than 1.65 billion members worldwide posting regularly about their behavior, Facebook is planning to take a more direct role in stopping suicide. On Tuesday, in the biggest step by a major technology company to incorporate suicide prevention tools into its platform, the social network introduced mechanisms and processes to make it easier for people to help friends who post messages about suicide or self-harm. With the new features, people can flag friends' posts that they deem suicidal; the posts will be reviewed by a team at the social network that will then provide language to communicate with the person who is at risk, as well as information on suicide prevention.

The timing coincides with a surge in suicide rates in the United States to a 30-year high. The increase has been particularly steep among women and middle-aged Americans, reflecting widespread desperation. Last year, President Obama declared a World Suicide Prevention Day in September, calling on people to recognize mental health issues early and to reach out to support one another.

Facebook has long thrust itself into major societal debates because of its vast reach and the enormous diversity of human behavior it sees."

I personally made some comments on Facebook about my brother taking his life and I was blown away by how many people reached out to me from my hometown. I wrote:

I was overwhelmed by all the people that reached out to me yesterday about the subject of suicide and my own brother. Back then, when my brother did that, our family felt like we were the only ones in the neighborhood that had to deal with that subject. I remember feeling that loneliness because it was such an odd thing. What I learned yesterday through private messages is that we were not the only family that dealt with this event. We were not alone. We just did not know that. The subject of mental illness is taboo, but many of us deal with different levels of it. Three days after Hurricane Andrew my stepfather's schizophrenic mother burnt down the house, I grew up in on Gulfstream Dr. in Miramar. So our family was hit with mental illness like it was a hurricane. When I left Miramar all those years ago and lost contact with so many people, I grew up with Sunshine Elementary, Perry Middle, and Miramar High School, I was leaving behind the memories of my brother, the ashes of my family home, and all the pain. I guess I did not realize back then that because of changing demographics, I would never be able to return to my hometown. At least not in the form it once was. I guess I never realize that all of you lost your hometown too. It does not make us racist to say out loud that the town we grew up in is gone forever and that, unlike so many other people across the country, our hometown only exists in the hearts and minds of the people that grew up there in the 1970s & 1980s. Last night I was reminded of what a community I really did grow up in and how freaking lucky I was or we were. I grew up with the greatest group of people a guy could ask for. I grew up in a town, that was by any metric, the coolest place in the country to have come of age in. Thank you for all your comments last night and to one special lady who reached out, and you know who you were, your dad and my brother were people who were dealing with mental health issues and they just needed help that did not get to them in time. If anyone is out there now reading this and is struggling, I say to you, reach out, reach out to someone somewhere. Don't give up.

So, I personally used Facebook to work through the effects of suicide with family members that are left behind. The fact that Facebook was now taking it a step further will in fact save lives. It is an example of what good social media can do and how technology has both positive and negative traits. Anything that can help turn the tide of the rising suicide rate is good in my mind. Collectively our society has a problem and only together are we going to solve it.

Facebook's new suicide prevention tools begin with a drop-down menu that allows people to report posts, that feature was previously only available to just English-speaking users. People across the globe can now flag a post as one that could raise concern about potential suicide; those posts will then come to the attention of Facebook's global community operations team for help 24 hours a day, seven days a week.

Posts flagged as possible suicide notes are to be expedited and reviewed faster by the team members, who also examine posts that Facebook users have reported as objectionable. Their staff has received special training about suicide Facebook claims.

CHAPTER TEN

The Birth and Impact of America's 988 Mental Emergency Call Center

In recent years, mental health has emerged as a critical issue globally, transcending borders, cultures, and socioeconomic backgrounds. Recognizing the need for immediate support for individuals facing mental health crises, America established the 988 Mental Emergency Call Center. This groundbreaking initiative has played a pivotal role in transforming the way mental health is perceived and managed in the country. This chapter delves into the inception, functions, achievements, challenges, and prospects of the 988 Mental Emergency Call Center.

Inception and Purpose: The 988 Mental Emergency Call Center was established with the primary objective of offering a dedicated helpline for individuals experiencing mental health emergencies. The number '988' was chosen to create a memorable and easily accessible helpline for individuals seeking immediate assistance during times of crisis.

Services Offered: The 988 Mental Emergency Call Center is staffed by trained volunteers and mental health professionals who provide round-the-clock emotional support and crisis intervention. Callers can expect empathetic and non-judgmental assistance, irrespective of their age, background, or mental health condition. The services offered by the center include:

1. **Crisis Intervention:** Trained professionals are available to engage with callers in a supportive manner, de-escalating crises and offering coping strategies.

2. **Emotional Support:** Call center volunteers offer a listening ear to individuals who may feel isolated or overwhelmed, providing a space to express their feelings and concerns.

3. **Referrals and Information:** The center provides information about available mental health resources, treatment options, and support services.

4. **Suicide Prevention:** One of the center's key focuses is suicide prevention. Trained staff are equipped to recognize warning signs and intervene effectively to provide immediate help.

5. **Follow-up Services:** The center aims to ensure continuity of care by following up with callers and connecting them to appropriate ongoing support.

Statistics and Achievements: Since its inception, the 988 Mental Emergency Call Center has achieved significant milestones, illustrating its impact on mental health crisis management in America:

1. **Call Volume:** The call center has received a consistently increasing number of calls each year, indicating a growing awareness of its services and a willingness to seek help with mental health concerns.

2. **Response Time:** The center prides itself on its rapid response time, ensuring that callers receive

assistance promptly during their moments of crisis.

3. **Suicide Prevention:** The center's interventions have been instrumental in preventing numerous suicides, underscoring the vital role it plays in saving lives.

4. **Public Awareness:** The establishment of the 988 helplines has contributed to raising public awareness about mental health issues, reducing stigma, and encouraging open conversations.

5. **Collaborations:** The center has collaborated with various mental health organizations, government agencies, and community partners to expand its reach and impact.

Challenges and Future Prospects: While the 988 Mental Emergency Call Center has undoubtedly made significant strides in promoting mental health well-being, it continues to face challenges that warrant attention:

1. **Resource Allocation:** Adequate funding and resources are essential to sustain and enhance the center's operations, training programs, and outreach initiatives.

2. **Stigma Reduction:** Despite progress, the stigma surrounding mental health remains a barrier. Continued efforts are needed to normalize seeking help for mental health issues.

3. **Capacity Building:** As call volumes increase, ensuring enough trained volunteers and mental health professionals is crucial.

4. **Cultural Sensitivity:** Tailoring services to address the diverse cultural and linguistic needs of the American population is vital for effective crisis intervention.

5. **Technology Integration:** Exploring the integration of technology, such as online chat and mobile applications, could expand the center's accessibility and reach.

The inception of the 988 Mental Emergency Call Center marks a significant milestone in America's approach to mental health crisis management. By providing a dedicated helpline for individuals facing mental health emergencies, the center has saved lives, reduced stigma, and fostered a more compassionate society. Despite challenges, its achievements serve as a testament to the transformative power of community-driven initiatives in addressing critical societal issues. The future holds immense potential for the 988 Mental Emergency Call Center to continue evolving, shaping a more empathetic and resilient America.

CHAPTER ELEVEN

When we think of all of the reasons why someone would take their own life, we think they are sick. After all, anyone who kills themselves must have something wrong with them, right? However, throughout time there are always people who do this act that leaves behind people who are utterly shocked. No one saw it coming, there were no signs. Sometimes people just saw the person just before the suicide and did not see any signs at all of something is wrong. So is there a thing where someone kills themselves in their right mind? Are there examples of clear-thinking people who just happen to do this thing? Is everyone who commits suicide nuts or out of their minds? Can somebody in proper mental health take their own life? Well, I know that end-of-life assisted suicides might fall into this category. There is an ongoing debate in this country about whether it is right to help a suffering person kill themselves. We all know the famous story of Dr. Jack Kevorkian. Physician-assisted suicide in the United States is legal in the states of California, Oregon, Vermont, and Washington. Clearly, these suicides are of a different nature.

Is there any form of suicide that makes sense? I'm not sure what the answer to that question is. Does anybody sound clear-minded and poignant before they take their own lives?

CHAPTER TWELVE

Depending on the study it is said that ninety percent of victims who kill themselves have some form of mental illness at the time of their death. Untreated depression is said to be the number one cause of suicide in America. Mental illness such as depression, Borderline Personality Disorder, Bi-polar Disorder, and Schizophrenia is the main cause of suicides.

There are also people who are genetically predisposed to depression. For some, it is passed down in their genes. It is rare that people die of suicide because of one reason. In most cases there are several causes, and not just one, for taking one's life.

The medical community now believes there are several factors that determine how susceptible a person is to suicidal thinking and behavior. These might include anything from an eating disorder to sexual abuse. Drugs or alcohol might be involved. There seem to be countless ever-expanding causes for suicide even including being victims of bullying and low self-esteem.

For me with all of the research I have now done on this subject. I am left with the heavy burden of trying to make sense of it all. I wanted to understand the subject better so maybe I could work through my own pain. My brother's suicide affected me in ways I never really realized. I wanted to see if I can help myself and help others out there that might be going through the same kind of confusion. I never seem to get away from this nightmare no matter how much time passes. Maybe that is the key. Maybe I am here to tell you reading this book, that you are not alone. Tell you that other people are out here who understand. To give it to you straight when people who do not know tell you it gets better over time. It does not.

Could it be that the help this book provides is to let you know that it never goes away? That there are good days and bad days, but there is never a day you completely escape from its grip. Maybe, if there is just one person who did not know about the 988-crisis line and their life is saved, then maybe, just maybe I've done something here.

R.I.P.

In Loving Memory of "Keith Michael Walker"
and "Anthony Comparetto" (aka "AC")